# A VERY VEGAN CHRISTMAS

**Recipes to celebrate food, save lives and protect our planet**

**By Maryanne Hall**

## Viva!

# CONTENTS

# INTRODUCTION

Ah, Christmas! A chance to gather with loved ones, force down a few mince pies, and pretend you actually enjoy your uncle's stories. But hey, it's also a chance to eat well, celebrate traditions (the tolerable ones, at least), and, if you're feeling adventurous, consider trying a vegan Christmas.

Imagine a table not groaning under the weight of yet another turkey surrounded by pigs in blankets, but decked out with some seriously incredible starters, mains (that won't make you question your life choices), and sides that will actually get eaten. Add in a few seasonal veggies, some incredible desserts that'll make you forget about the brandy butter, and naturally, something boozy to wash it all down. Whether you're going full tradition or feeling a bit wild, this guide's got you covered.

So, why not shake things up with a cruelty-free Christmas? It's a chance to eat in a way that reflects the season's joyful message of giving, sharing and caring for all living beings. Sound good? Let's get into it.

## ABOUT VIVA!

Viva! is the UK's leading vegan charity, and we've been investigating, campaigning, and generally shaking things up when it comes to how our diets impact animals, the planet, and our own health for 30 years! We present talks and cookery demos, and run the Vegan Recipe Club (a free app and website), leaflets and merchandise to support people on their journeys towards kinder, sustainable and healthy diets.
**viva.org.uk**

## ABOUT VEGAN RECIPE CLUB

Vegan Recipe Club is your one-stop-shop for recipes that won't leave you missing meat. Brought to you by Viva!, we've spent the last three decades gathering a solid collection of plant-based recipes that even your fussiest family member will like. With hundreds of thousands of social media followers and partnerships with chefs, influencers, and brands, we're all about showing you just how easy (and tasty) a vegan diet can be.
**veganrecipeclub.org.uk**

# PICKY BITS AND STARTERS

# SMOKED 'SALMON' BLINIS

Prep time: **15 minutes**  |  Cook time: **5 minutes**  |  Serves: **makes 28 blinis (approx.)**

Wow your guests with this spectacular vegan version of a traditional
Christmas starter – well worth the effort.

## INGREDIENTS

### VEGAN SMOKED SALMON
Use shop-bought vegan smoked salmon if
short of time
- **2 large carrots, peeled then sliced into
  thick ribbons using a vegetable peeler**

### MARINADE
- **1 tsp white miso paste**
- **4 tbsp neutral oil (eg rapeseed)**
- **¼ tsp salt**
- **2 tsp syrup (eg maple or agave)**
- **1 tsp smoked paprika**
- **1 tbsp lemon juice**
- **1 nori sheet, cut into 4 strips or 1 tsp
  nori flakes**

### BLINIS
- **125g plain white flour**
- **¼ tsp bicarbonate of soda**
- **1 tsp baking powder**
- **2 tsp caster sugar**
- **½ tsp salt**
- **200ml unsweetened plant milk
  (we like soya)**
- **½ tsp lemon juice**

### TOPPINGS
- **Vegan cream cheese (best to use a
  high-quality cream cheese for this one)**
- **Capers**
- **Fresh dill or finely chopped chives**
- **Red onion, finely diced or finely sliced**
- **Cucumber ribbons**
- **Sliced avocado**
- **Lemon wedges and/or lemon zest**

## INSTRUCTIONS

### VEGAN SMOKED SALMON
1. Steam the carrot ribbons for about 5 minutes.
   Check them after 3-4 minutes because you
   don't want them to get soggy! They need to
   be very lightly cooked. Let the carrots cool a
   little bit but use while still warm.

### MARINADE
1. Using a medium-sized bowl, stir all the
   ingredients together thoroughly.
2. Place the warm (ish) carrot ribbons into the
   marinade and mix well without mashing up
   the carrot.
3. Put the carrot and the marinade in an airtight
   container and leave to absorb the flavours for
   a minimum of 2 hours.
4. If using nori sheets, remove them before
   serving.

### BLINIS
1. In a large mixing bowl, thoroughly combine all
   the ingredients until smooth.
2. Using a large frying pan, on a medium heat,
   cover the surface with a good glug of oil.
3. Take the blini batter and place teaspoon-
   sized blobs into the pan, leaving a couple of
   centimetres between each one.
4. Fry each blini for 2 minutes on each side,
   remove them from the pan and leave to cool.
   Repeat this step until all the batter has been
   used up.

### TOPPINGS/ASSEMBLY
1. Top each blini with a teaspoon of vegan
   cream cheese, a ribbon of vegan smoked
   salmon and the toppings of your choice.

# EASY FESTIVE PÂTÉ

**Prep time: 10 minutes** | Chill time: **60 minutes** | Serves: **6 as a starter**

Viva!'s Dr Justine Butler developed this simple recipe when she had to cook Christmas dinner for a French friend – needless to say they loved it!

## INGREDIENTS

- 200g smoked tofu, drained and patted dry
- 100g cashew pieces, soaked for a minimum of an hour or boiled for 15 minutes, drained and rinsed
- 3 tbsp rapeseed oil
- 1 tbsp ground almonds
- Juice of 1 lemon
- ½ tsp smoked paprika
- A few drops of liquid smoke (optional)
- 2 tsp cognac (use brandy if you don't have cognac)
- ½ tsp freshly ground black pepper
- ½ tsp salt
- 1½ tbsp vegan butter
- ½ tsp turmeric

## INSTRUCTIONS

1. Blend everything except the butter and turmeric until smooth.
2. Spoon into small pots and smooth the top down.
3. Melt the butter in a small saucepan on a low heat, then stir in the turmeric until it has dissolved.
4. Pour a little of the melted butter onto the top of the pâté in each pot then chill in the fridge for at least an hour before serving.

### SERVING SUGGESTIONS
Celery sticks, chutney, crackers, crusty baguette, fresh herbs, fruit, garlic bread, gherkins, pickled onions, pink peppercorns, warm bread

# BAKED 'CAMEMBERT' PARCEL WITH CRANBERRY BURST

Prep time: **5 minutes** | Cook time: **25 minutes** | Serves: **6 (as a starter)**

Delicious, oozing, rich and creamy vegan 'Camembert' encased in a golden pastry parcel with a cranberry burst.

## INGREDIENTS

- 350g vegan ready-to-roll puff pastry block
- 4 tbsp cranberry sauce, apricot jam, blackcurrant jam, fig jam, redcurrant jelly or quince jelly
- 140g-250g whole vegan 'Camembert', 'Brie' or other similar vegan cheese (any shape is fine)
- 1 tbsp unsweetened plant milk mixed with 2 tsp syrup (eg maple or agave) for brushing

## INSTRUCTIONS

1. Preheat the oven to 190°C/375°F/Gas Mark 5.

2. Dust a clean surface with plain flour, cut the pastry in half and roll out both sheets to around 3mm thick.

3. Spoon the cranberry sauce into the centre of one of the pastry sheets (making sure you cover about 4cm wider than the vegan cheese). Place the vegan cheese on top of the cranberry sauce and then place the other sheet of pastry on top of that. You can trim the pastry around the shape of the 'cheese' – again making sure there's around 4cm excess around the edge.

4. Press the two pastry sheets together firmly then use a fork to press down the edges to seal it and make it look nice.

5. Using the leftover puff pastry you can add a pretty shape with a pastry cutter (eg a star or a Christmas tree).

6. Lightly brush the pastry all over with the plant milk/syrup mix.

7. Place in the oven and bake for 20-25 minutes. Check after 15 and if it is darkening on the top, cover with foil or greaseproof paper. Leave the pastry to sit for a few minutes before serving. Take care to catch the cheesy filling as it oozes out.

### SERVING SUGGESTIONS
Baby carrots, celery, crackers, crusty bread, fresh rosemary, fresh thyme, garlic bread, grapes, olives, pecans, pomegranate, raw broccoli, raw cauliflower, salted mixed nuts, sliced apple, walnuts

# CAULIFLOWER & CHESTNUT SOUP WITH CHEESY APPLE CROUTONS

**Prep time: 10 minutes** | Cook time: **20 minutes** | Serves: **4**

This delectable, savoury soup makes the perfect festive starter or Boxing Day lunch.

## INGREDIENTS

### SOUP

- 1 large white onion, finely diced
- 2 cloves garlic, finely chopped
- 1 large cauliflower, cut into florets
- 250ml unsweetened plant milk
- 850ml vegan stock
- 2 tbsp vegan sherry or vegan white wine (optional)
- 150ml vegan double cream (don't need to whip) or vegan crème fraîche
- 200g vacuum-packed chestnuts, roughly chopped
- ¼ tsp black pepper
- Salt, to taste

### CROUTONS

- 8 slices of baguette (around 2cm thick)
- 200g vegan cheddar-style cheese, grated
- 50g dried apple (optional), finely chopped

**Optional toppings:** drizzle of olive oil, drizzle of truffle oil, fresh herbs, our sage crisps (see page 27), roasted cauliflower, roasted chickpeas, toasted chopped chestnuts, toasted mixed seeds, vegan cream

## INSTRUCTIONS

### SOUP

1. Heat a tablespoon of oil in a large saucepan then add the onion. Lightly fry on a medium heat until soft then add the garlic and fry for a further couple of minutes.

2. Add the cauliflower, plant milk and stock. Bring to the boil then simmer on a medium heat for 10-12 minutes or until the cauliflower is tender.

3. Pour in the sherry, vegan cream, chestnuts and black pepper and bring to the boil for a few minutes.

4. Take off the heat and then blend with a stick blender or transfer to a high-speed blender until smooth (if using a blender, leave to cool slightly before taking off the lid). Taste the soup and add salt if required.

### CROUTONS

1. Heat the grill to medium-high then toast the bread on both sides.

2. Mix the cheese with the dried apple and evenly distribute over the top of the croutons. Grill until melted and golden. Serve with the soup.

# THE MAIN EVENT

# NO TURKEY FESTIVE ROAST

Prep time: **20 minutes**  |  Cook time: **80 minutes**  |  Serves: **4-6**

This mouth-watering no turkey roast is much easier to make than it looks! With a crispy 'skin' and juicy, tender middle, you'll create a dazzling centrepiece for your festive table.

## INGREDIENTS

### NO TURKEY ROAST
- 3 cloves garlic, finely chopped
- 400g firm tofu, drained
- 3 tbsp nutritional yeast
- 2 tbsp white miso paste
- 2 tsp onion powder
- 1 vegan stock cube mixed with 6 tbsp boiling water
- 1 tbsp lemon juice
- 1 tbsp syrup (eg maple or agave)
- 1½ tsp salt
- ¼ tsp black pepper
- ½ tsp dried rosemary
- ½ tsp dried sage
- 60g chickpeas, drained and rinsed
- 50g chickpea flour
- 310g vital wheat gluten flour

### NO TURKEY ROAST RUB
- 5 tbsp vegan butter, melted
- ¼-½ tsp salt
- 1 tsp (heaped) soft brown sugar
- 1 tsp dried thyme
- 1 tsp dried sage
- 1 tsp dried rosemary
- 1 tsp dried tarragon (optional)
- ½ tsp garlic powder
- ½ tsp onion powder
- 1 tsp paprika

### NO TURKEY ROAST SKIN
- Rice paper sheets (buy in supermarkets, online and in global supermarkets) to fully cover the vegan turkey with a single layer

## INSTRUCTIONS

### NO TURKEY ROAST
1. Fry the garlic for two minutes then place all of the ingredients, apart from the chickpea flour and vital wheat gluten flour, into the food processor using the regular blade (s-blade) and blend until very smooth.

2. Keeping the same regular blade, add the chickpea flour and vital wheat gluten flour and blend for around 30 seconds until the ingredients have combined and formed a smooth dough. Don't overstir.

3. Remove the dough and, without kneading, form into a smooth ball.

4. Securely wrap the ball of dough in no more than two layers of tin foil and place into a large metal steamer basket with the lid on. Steam for 25 minutes on medium-high before turning the roast over and steaming for another 25 minutes. You might need to add more water to the steamer.

5. Whilst the dough is steaming, preheat the oven to 180°C/350°F/Gas Mark 4 and before the end of steaming, make the no turkey roast rub.

### NO TURKEY ROAST RUB
1. Using a small saucepan, mix all the ingredients on a low heat until the butter has melted.

### NO TURKEY ROAST SKIN/ASSEMBLY
1. Remove the no turkey roast from the steamer and thoroughly coat in half of the no turkey roast rub.

2. Dip the rice paper sheets in hot water until soft and rehydrated. Coat the no turkey roast in the rice paper sheets in a single layer, making sure there are no gaps (it helps to overlap the edges of the sheets).

3. Place the no turkey roast in the oven for 10 minutes. Remove from the oven and evenly coat with the remaining no turkey roast rub. Place back into the oven and cook for another 15-20 minutes or until the skin is nicely golden and crispy. If the skin is browning too quickly, cover with foil.

**TIP**
—
Make sure you use firm tofu, not extra-firm or silken.

# CHESTNUT, MUSHROOM & RED WINE PITHIVIER

Prep time: **15 minutes**  |  Cook time: **1 hour**  |  Serves: **8**

This traditional French dish, with its sunbeam pastry, is a feast for the eyes – rich, tasty and easy to create.

## INGREDIENTS

### FILLING
- 1 red onion, finely diced
- 2 leeks, ends removed and finely sliced
- 400g button mushrooms, halved
- 3 cloves garlic, finely chopped
- ½ tsp cayenne pepper
- 50g plain flour
- 2 tbsp tomato purée (or use harissa paste for a bit of spice)
- 200g vacuum-packed chestnuts, roughly chopped
- 2 tomatoes, roughly chopped
- 10 sun-dried tomatoes, finely chopped
- 1 tbsp dried or fresh thyme, stalks removed and finely chopped
- ½ tbsp dried or fresh rosemary or oregano, stalks removed and finely chopped
- 2 tbsp balsamic vinegar
- 175ml vegan red wine (use alcohol-free if preferred or mix 1 tbsp red miso paste with 175ml boiling water)
- 250ml vegan stock
- 1 tbsp soft brown sugar
- 250g pre-cooked quinoa or lentils
- Salt and pepper, to taste

## INSTRUCTIONS

### FILLING
1. Fry the onion on a medium heat in a little vegan butter or oil until golden.
2. Add the leeks and fry for a further 5 minutes.
3. Add the mushrooms and fry for another 5 minutes.
4. Stir in the garlic and the cayenne pepper and fry for 2 minutes.
5. Stir through the flour until all the vegetables have been covered.
6. Stir through the tomato purée and add all of the other ingredients apart from the pre-cooked quinoa/lentils.
7. Allow the mixture to simmer, stirring regularly, for around 15-20 minutes or until the liquid has reduced down significantly (you don't want the mixture to be too runny).
8. Add the quinoa or lentils to the mix and stir through. The consistency should be thick so that it stays upright. Add a little more stock if necessary (you don't want it to be runny). Set aside until needed.

## INGREDIENTS CONT.

### PASTRY
- 640g vegan ready-to-use puff pastry sheets
- 2 tbsp unsweetened plant milk mixed with 1 tbsp syrup (eg maple or agave) for brushing

## INSTRUCTIONS CONT.

### PASTRY
1. Preheat the oven to 190°C/375°F/Gas Mark 5 (ensure it's fully preheated).
2. Line a large baking tray with greaseproof paper and set aside.
3. On a floured surface, use a large dinner plate to cut one of the pastry sheets around the shape of the plate (this is your small pastry circle).
4. Place the smaller circle on the lined baking tray and set aside.
5. Take the next pastry sheet and again cut around the shape of the plate but this time leave 2cm of extra pastry around the edge (this is your large pastry circle).

### ASSEMBLY
1. Transfer the mixture onto the small pastry circle and heap the mixture as high as possible, leaving at least 5cm of pastry free around the edge.
2. Cover the mixture with the large pastry circle and seal the edges with your fingers. Brush the edges with some oil.
3. To create the sun pattern, make a tiny hole in the top centre and then score wavy lines deeply (but not all the way through!) from the centre to the outer edge of the pastry using a sharp knife.
4. Brush the outside of the pastry with the plant milk/syrup mix until fully coated.
5. Place in the oven and bake for 25-30 minutes or until crisp and golden.

CHESTNUT, MUSHROOM
& RED WINE PITHIVIER

NUT ROAST WREATH
WITH SAGE CRISPS

# NUT ROAST WREATH WITH SAGE CRISPS

Prep time: **20 minutes** | Cook time: **50 minutes** | Serves: **6**

Viva!'s Campaigns Manager said this was the nicest nut roast he'd ever eaten! Bursting with flavour, nutty deliciousness and a lovely moist texture – who said nut roast was boring?!

## INGREDIENTS

### NUT ROAST

- 2 tbsp vegan butter
- 1 red onion, diced
- ½ leek, sliced
- 1 carrot, finely diced
- 3 cloves garlic, finely sliced
- 100g mushrooms, diced
- 100g puy lentils, cooked and drained (or use ready-to-use)
- 150g vacuum-packed chestnuts, roughly chopped (you can chop these with the mixed nuts in the food processor)
- 200g mixed nuts (we like a combination of macadamias, cashews and pistachios), roughly chopped by hand or in the food processor (use the pulse function to avoid them becoming too powdery/fine, or use pre-chopped nuts if preferred)
- 50g dried cranberries or apricots, chopped
- 8 sun-dried tomatoes, roughly chopped with scissors
- 150g breadcrumbs (ideally wholemeal – homemade or shop-bought)
- 1 tbsp tomato purée
- 2 tsp yeast extract
- 1 tbsp syrup (eg maple or agave)
- 300ml vegan stock (use 1 stock cube in 300ml boiling water)
- Juice and zest of 1 orange
- ½ tsp ground nutmeg
- ½ tsp allspice
- 2 tsp dried or fresh rosemary, finely chopped

## INSTRUCTIONS

### NUT ROAST

1. Preheat the oven to 180°C/350°F/Gas Mark 4.
2. Using a large frying pan or wok, heat the vegan butter on a medium heat and sweat the onion, leeks, carrot and garlic until soft.
3. Stir through the mushrooms and heat for 5 minutes, stirring frequently.
4. Add the lentils, chestnuts, mixed nuts, cranberries, sun-dried tomatoes, breadcrumbs, tomato purée, yeast extract, syrup and stock.
5. Continue to heat on medium until the stock has absorbed, stirring occasionally.
6. Once the stock has absorbed, add the orange juice and zest, nutmeg, allspice, rosemary, thyme, nutritional yeast, flax egg, salt and pepper and combine.
7. Thoroughly coat the inside of a 24cm non-stick bundt/ring cake/decorative tin with a neutral oil (eg rapeseed) then pour in the nut roast mixture, spreading evenly. Press the mixture down firmly.
8. Place a ring of greaseproof paper or foil over the top of the nut roast to stop it browning too quickly.
9. Place in the oven and cook for 30-35 minutes or until golden and firm. If it's not firming up, check after 30 minutes, remove the greaseproof paper ring and bake until golden/firm (but not dried out).
10. After removing from the oven, allow the nut roast to cool slightly before turning it out of the tin.

## INGREDIENTS CONT.

- 1 tbsp dried or fresh thyme leaves
- 2 tbsp nutritional yeast
- 2 tbsp ground flaxseed mixed with 4 tbsp warm water (this is your flax egg. Use port instead of water if you're feeling fancy – thank you Dr Justine Butler for this tip!)
- 1-2 tsp salt
- ¼ tsp black pepper

### SAGE CRISPS

- Vegetable oil for frying
- 20g fresh sage leaves, stalks removed
- Salt

## INSTRUCTIONS CONT.

### SAGE CRISPS

1. Heat approx. 1cm depth of oil in a medium-sized saucepan on a medium-high heat.

2. Wait until the oil has fully heated up before adding the sage leaves in batches. Fry them for 30 seconds to 1 minute before removing them with a slotted spoon. Place on kitchen roll.

3. Repeat the process until all the sage leaves have been fried then very lightly sprinkle with salt.

### SERVING SUGGESTIONS

Boiled potatoes, celeriac gratin, cranberry sauce, gravy (see page 51), mashed potatoes, mushroom sauce (see page 52), roast potatoes, roasted vegetables, steamed vegetables, vegan cauliflower cheese, vegan dauphinoise potatoes, vegan stuffing, vegan Yorkshire puddings, vegetable crisps

# BUTTERNUT, WALNUT & BLUE 'CHEESE' FILO PIE

Prep time: **20 minutes** | Cook time: **65 minutes** | Serves: **6**

This crispy golden pie not only looks impressive but it's easy to make.
A firm favourite in the Viva! office and perfect for a festive feast.

## INGREDIENTS

- **1kg butternut squash, peeled, deseeded and cut into 1cm cubes**
- **2 red onions, finely diced**
- **130g walnuts, roughly chopped**
- **2 cloves garlic, finely chopped**
- **½ tsp dried chilli flakes**
- **200g oyster or mixed mushrooms (or any mushrooms of your choice), sliced**
- **400g fresh spinach**
- **2 tsp syrup (eg maple or agave)**
- **1 tbsp lemon juice (fresh or bottled)**
- **1½ tsp salt**
- **¼ tsp black pepper**
- **100g vegan butter, melted**
- **6 sheets filo pastry**
- **150g vegan blue cheese, cubed**

## INSTRUCTIONS

1. Preheat the oven to 180°C/350°F/Gas Mark 4.
2. Place the squash cubes on a large baking tray, thoroughly coat with oil (you might want to get your hands in there!) and bake for 20 minutes or until soft (but not mushy or caramelised), turning once.
3. While the squash is roasting, using a large frying pan with a lid, fry the onions and walnuts in a little oil and cook for 5 minutes, stirring frequently. Add the garlic and chilli flakes and cook for a further 2 minutes.
4. Pour the mixture into a large mixing bowl and set aside.
5. Place the frying pan back on the heat with a little more oil. Add the mushrooms and fry for around 3 minutes, stirring frequently. Add the mushrooms to the mixing bowl with the onions, walnuts and garlic and set aside.
6. Meanwhile, put the spinach in a colander placed over the sink. Pour over a kettleful of boiling water to wilt. Thoroughly squeeze out the excess water then chop the spinach into smaller pieces before adding to the mixing bowl.
7. When the squash has cooked, add it to the mixing bowl then add the syrup, lemon juice, salt and pepper and thoroughly combine. Set aside.
8. Grease a 22cm springform tin with vegan butter. Using a pastry brush, thoroughly coat 1 sheet of filo pastry with the melted butter and line the base of the tin, leaving an overhang. Repeat with 4 more sheets (thoroughly coating each sheet in the melted butter), layering each one at different angles for folding up later.
9. Fill the pastry case with half the vegetable mixture followed by half the vegan blue cheese. Add the remaining mixture and top with the vegan blue cheese. Fold the final filo sheet in half and use to cover the filling. Fold over the overhanging pastry and scrunch up the ends.
10. Brush the top with the melted butter and bake for 45 minutes or until golden and crisp. Check after 25 minutes and if the top is browning too quickly, cover with tin foil.

# SIDES AND TRIMMINGS

# THE ULTIMATE ROAST POTATOES

Prep time: **10 minutes** | Cook time: **1 hour** | Serves: **4**

Beautifully golden, crispy on the outside, fluffy on the inside and infused with garlic and rosemary – need we say more?!

## INGREDIENTS

- **1kg good roasting potatoes (eg Maris Piper), peeled and cut into chunks**
- **5 tbsp rapeseed or olive oil**
- **Salt**
- **Handful of fresh rosemary sprigs**
- **Bulb of garlic, broken up into individual cloves (keep the skin on)**

## INSTRUCTIONS

1. Preheat the oven to 200°C/390°F/Gas Mark 6.
2. Add the potatoes and some salt to a large saucepan. Bring to the boil and then simmer on medium-high for 10 minutes.
3. Drain the potatoes and then fluff them up in the colander by shaking it back and forth.
4. Leave them to dry in the colander, or ideally in a single layer on a baking rack, for 10-20 minutes if you have time (this allows the potatoes to develop a crust which goes nice and crispy in the oven).
5. Place the oil in the roasting tin then pop it in the oven for a few minutes.
6. Once the oil is smoking hot, remove the tray and add the potatoes gently but quickly, using a spatula to turn them over so they're completely covered in oil. Sprinkle with salt and then place them in the oven for 25 minutes.
7. After 25 minutes, remove from the oven and turn them all over. Add the garlic cloves and rosemary (evenly spaced) then return the pan to the oven for another 20-30 minutes or until golden and crispy.

# LEMON BRUSSELS SPROUTS

Prep time: **5 minutes** | Cook time: **40 minutes** | Serves: **4**

Poor old Brussels sprouts have a hard time impressing people but we think we might just have cracked it with this scrumptious recipe.

## INGREDIENTS

- **500g Brussels sprouts, ends removed and halved**
- **3 onions, peeled and quartered**
- **Zest of ½ a lemon**
- **Handful of thyme sprigs**
- **½ tsp chilli flakes**
- **Salt and pepper, to taste**
- **2 tbsp vegan Parmesan (optional)**
- **Juice of ½ a lemon**

## INSTRUCTIONS

1. Preheat the oven to 190°C/375°F/Gas Mark 5.

2. In a large roasting tin, thoroughly mix the Brussels sprouts, onions, lemon zest, thyme sprigs, chilli flakes and salt and pepper with a good glug of oil (you might want to get your hands in there!).

3. Roast for 20 minutes, turn the sprouts and then sprinkle over the vegan Parmesan. Place the sprouts back in the oven for a further 10-20 minutes or until they are crispy and golden.

4. Once cooked, evenly coat the sprouts in the lemon juice and serve.

# CRISPY MAPLE ROASTED PARSNIPS

Prep time: **10 minutes** | Cook time: **40 minutes** | Serves: **4**

Who doesn't love sweet, soft and sticky roasted parsnips? This recipe brings out their rich, nutty flavour.

## INGREDIENTS

- 1kg of parsnips, peeled and cut lengthways into 4
- 8 tbsp neutral oil (eg rapeseed)
- Salt and black pepper
- 4 bay leaves
- 4 tbsp maple syrup
- 2 tsp red wine vinegar

## INSTRUCTIONS

1. Preheat the oven to 180°C/350°F/Gas Mark 4.
2. Cook the peeled parsnips in a pan of salted boiling water for 5 minutes, then drain and steam dry.
3. Using a large roasting tray, tip in the parsnips then thoroughly coat with the oil and a sprinkling of salt and pepper (you might want to get your hands in there!). Arrange in a single layer then roast for 30 minutes, turning once.
4. Mix the syrup and the vinegar together.
5. Remove the tray from the oven then distribute the bay leaves over the parsnips and drizzle with the vinegar and maple syrup mix. Thoroughly and evenly coat then place back in the oven for a further 10 minutes or until crispy and golden.

# STICKY CIDER & ORANGE CARROTS

Prep time: **10 minutes** | Cook time: **35 minutes** | Serves: **4 (as a side)**

Dr Justine Butler's carrot recipe is simple yet delectable, making it the perfect addition to your Christmas table.

## INGREDIENTS

- 2 tbsp vegan butter
- 3 large carrots, trimmed, peeled and chopped into finger-sized pieces
- 2 tbsp fresh orange juice
- 2 tbsp cider
- 1 tsp brown sugar
- ¼ tsp salt
- ⅛ tsp black pepper
- 1 tbsp thyme leaves, stalks removed
- Handful of toasted pine nuts (optional)

## INSTRUCTIONS

1. Melt the butter in a large frying pan on a low heat. Then add the carrots and cook for 10-15 minutes, tossing occasionally until browned.

2. Add the orange juice, cider, sugar, salt, pepper and thyme and simmer for 15-20 minutes until the carrots are tender and sticky.

3. Stir through the toasted pine nuts and heat for 2 minutes.

4. Serve, or leave to cool then reheat when ready to use.

# TRADITIONAL BRAISED RED CABBAGE

Prep time: **10 minutes** | Cook time: **80 minutes** | Serves: **4**

A festive essential, this side dish is sweetly spiced, colourful and moreishly delicious.

## INGREDIENTS

- 2 tbsp vegan butter, plus extra to serve
- 1 red onion, finely sliced
- 1 cinnamon stick
- ¼ tsp ground cloves
- ¼ tsp ground nutmeg
- 1 red cabbage, cored and finely shredded
- 1 apple of your choice, peeled, cored and finely chopped
- 3 tbsp light muscovado sugar (or any soft brown sugar)
- 150ml balsamic vinegar
- 2 tbsp cranberry sauce
- 1 tsp salt
- ¼ tsp black pepper

## INSTRUCTIONS

1. Melt the butter in a large pan on a medium heat and add the onion. Fry for 5 minutes before adding the cinnamon, cloves and nutmeg. Heat for a further 2 minutes.

2. Stir through the cabbage, making sure it's well coated in the butter and spices.

3. Add the apple, sugar and vinegar, reduce the heat to low, stir well. Cover and cook for 45 minutes, stirring occasionally.

4. Stir through the cranberry sauce, salt and pepper and cook for another 25 minutes. Stir through a tablespoon of vegan butter before serving.

# SAGE, ONION & HAZELNUT STUFFING

Prep time: **20 minutes** | Cook time: **70 minutes** | Serves: **4-6**

Of course you can cheat and buy a ready-made stuffing but it will never be the same as homemade. This recipe will fill your home with the comforting aromas of a traditional Christmas.

## INGREDIENTS

- 2 tbsp vegan butter
- 1 onion, diced
- 2 sticks celery, finely diced
- 150g mushrooms, diced (optional)
- 2 cloves garlic, crushed
- 100g hazelnuts, roughly chopped by hand or in the food processor (optional)
- 2 tbsp dried or fresh sage, finely chopped
- 2 tbsp fresh parsley, finely chopped
- 1 tbsp dried or fresh rosemary, finely chopped
- ½ tsp salt
- ¼ tsp black pepper
- 2 tbsp ground flaxseed mixed with 4 tbsp water (this is your flax egg)
- 400g slightly stale ciabatta or sourdough (ideally), crusts removed and cut into small cubes (once the crusts are removed the bread will weigh around 250g)
- 350ml hot vegan stock (1 vegan stock cube mixed with 350ml boiling water)

## INSTRUCTIONS

1. Preheat the oven to 180°C/350°F/Gas Mark 4.
2. Using a large frying pan or wok, heat the vegan butter on medium then fry the onion and celery until soft.
3. Add the mushrooms, garlic and hazelnuts and heat for a further 5 minutes.
4. Stir through the sage, parsley, rosemary, salt and pepper and heat for 2-3 minutes.
5. Remove from the heat and stir through the flax egg, bread and stock.
6. Transfer the mixture to a roasting tray (around 20cm x 20cm), press down and cover with foil. Bake in the oven for 30 minutes. Remove the foil, drizzle with a little oil (optional) then bake for a further 20 minutes or until golden.

### TIP
If you're using fresh bread instead of stale, preheat the oven to 130°C and spread the bread cubes out on a baking tray. Place in the oven to dry out for 20 minutes before removing and leaving to cool.

# CAULIFLOWER 'CHEESE'

Prep time: **10 minutes** | Cook time: **35 minutes** | Serves: **6**

We haven't scrimped on the sauce in this recipe – it's a flavour-packed béchamel topped off with gooey melted vegan cheese and crispy golden breadcrumbs. No Christmas dinner would be the same without it!

## INGREDIENTS

### CAULIFLOWER
- 1 large cauliflower, cut into florets

### BÉCHAMEL SAUCE
- 6 tbsp vegan butter/spread
- 6 tbsp plain flour
- 600ml unsweetened plant milk
- 1 tbsp English or Dijon mustard
- ¾ tsp ground or fresh nutmeg, grated
- 6 tbsp nutritional yeast
- 1½ tsp salt
- ½ tsp black pepper
- 50g vegan cheese, grated (optional)
- 2 tsp white wine vinegar (optional)

### TOPPING
- 200g vegan cheese, grated
- 6 tbsp breadcrumbs (optional – we like panko)

## INSTRUCTIONS

### CAULIFLOWER
1. Preheat the oven to 220°C/425°F/Gas Mark 7.
2. Bring a large saucepan of water to the boil, then add the cauliflower and continue to boil for 5 minutes if you like it with a bit of bite or 7 minutes if you like it a little softer. Take out a piece and check that it's cooked to your taste. You definitely don't want it to be mushy.
3. Drain the cauliflower then tip it into an ovenproof dish in a single layer. Set aside.

### BÉCHAMEL SAUCE
1. Using a large saucepan, melt the butter on a low heat.
2. Take the saucepan off the heat and stir in the flour until you have a smooth paste.
3. Return the pan to the heat, turn up to medium and very gradually add the plant milk, stirring continuously to avoid lumps.
4. Once the sauce has thickened, add the mustard, nutmeg, nutritional yeast, salt, pepper, vegan cheese and white wine vinegar. Use a balloon whisk to get rid of lumps if necessary.
5. Stir thoroughly then pour evenly over the cauliflower.

### TOPPING/ASSEMBLY
1. Evenly distribute the grated vegan cheese over the cauliflower then sprinkle over the breadcrumbs.
2. Place the dish into the oven and bake for 20 minutes or until golden and the vegan cheese has melted.

# EASY YORKSHIRE PUDDINGS

Prep time: **25 minutes** | Cook time: **20 minutes** | Serves: **6**

Get your Yorkshire pud fix with this very simple recipe! It is guaranteed to brighten up any Christmas spread without the fuss!

## INGREDIENTS

- Vegetable oil
- 190g self-raising flour
- ¾ tsp baking powder
- ¾ tsp salt
- 270ml unsweetened soya or almond milk

## INSTRUCTIONS

1. Preheat the oven to 215°C/420°F/Gas Mark 7.

2. Fill a 12-hole muffin tin with 2 tablespoons of vegetable oil in each hole.

3. Place the tray in the oven for 20 minutes to make sure the oil is super-hot!

4. After about 15 minutes of the oil heating, make the batter but only mix the ingredients together just before use.

5. Sieve the flour, salt and baking powder into a large mixing bowl. Gradually pour in the plant milk, whisking constantly.

6. Remove the heated oil from the oven and quickly pour 2 tablespoons of batter into each muffin hole. For the best shape, try to pour the batter continuously (you might want to measure the first one into a measuring cup then roughly copy the amount poured to make it quicker).

7. Put the tray straight back in the oven and cook for 20 minutes.

# SAUCES

# CARAMELISED ONION & RED WINE GRAVY

Prep time: **5 minutes** | Cook time: **20 minutes** | Serves: **4**

Everyone needs a delicious gravy recipe up their sleeve and trust us when we say that creating your own from scratch makes all the difference.

## INGREDIENTS

- 2 red onions, finely sliced
- 4 cloves garlic, finely chopped
- 1 tsp Dijon or English mustard
- 1 tsp yeast extract
- 2 tbsp plain white flour
- 100ml vegan red wine
- 450ml vegan stock
- 2 tbsp soy sauce
- 2 sprigs fresh thyme
- 1 sprig fresh rosemary
- ¼ tsp black pepper
- 2 tbsp cranberry sauce or redcurrant jelly

## INSTRUCTIONS

1. In a medium-sized saucepan, fry the onion in a little oil on a low heat until nicely caramelised (but not burnt). You might need to add a little extra oil.
2. Add the garlic and fry for another 2 minutes.
3. Stir in the mustard and yeast extract and heat for 2 minutes.
4. Add the flour and thoroughly combine with the other ingredients.
5. Pour in the wine, stock and soy sauce and add the thyme and rosemary. Bring to the boil then simmer for 10 minutes or until the gravy has thickened to your taste, stirring frequently.
6. Stir through the black pepper and cranberry sauce and heat for another 2 minutes.
7. Remove the rosemary and thyme sprigs before serving.
8. Either blend all the ingredients together until smooth, strain out the vegetables or keep it chunky.

# CREAMY WHITE WINE MUSHROOM SAUCE

Prep time: **5 minutes** | Cook time: **20 minutes** | Serves: **4**

This deliciously creamy sauce recipe goes perfectly with all of our sumptuous mains – your spread won't be the same without it!

## INGREDIENTS

- 1 tbsp vegan butter
- 1 onion, finely chopped
- 250g mushrooms, sliced
- ½ tsp salt
- ¼ tsp black pepper
- 1 clove garlic, finely chopped
- 150ml vegan dry white wine
- 150ml vegan cream
- 1 tsp lemon juice
- 1 tsp syrup (eg maple or agave) or brown sugar (optional)
- 1 tbsp parsley, stalks removed and finely chopped

## INSTRUCTIONS

1. Fry the onion in the vegan butter until soft.
2. Add the mushrooms, salt and pepper and cook until soft but before they released their juices.
3. Add the garlic and fry for a further 2 minutes.
4. Pour the white wine into the pan, bring to the boil and then simmer down until the liquid has reduced by half.
5. Stir through the vegan cream, lemon juice and syrup and heat for a further couple of minutes or until reduced down to your desired consistency.
6. Top with the fresh parsley.

# LEFTOVERS/
# THE DAY AFTER

# NO TURKEY BRIOCHE BUN WITH VEGAN CRACKLING & APPLE SAUCE

Prep time: **10 minutes** | Cook time: **15 minutes** | Serves: **4**

It's worth making an extra No Turkey Festive Roast just to create these sandwiches! The combination of crispy vegan crackling, succulent no turkey and sweet apple sauce is heavenly.

## INGREDIENTS

### FILLING
- **8 slices of no turkey roast (see page 20) or cook a shop-bought vegan roast**
- **130g vegan shop-bought stuffing or use our stuffing on page 43**

### APPLE SAUCE
Or use a shop-bought apple sauce
- **5 Bramley or Granny Smith apples, peeled, cored and sliced**
- **85g caster sugar**
- **85g vegan butter**

### VEGAN CRACKLING
(OPTIONAL)
- **Rapeseed oil for frying**
- **Fresh or dried bean curd skin/yuba sheets (don't use the really crispy dried sheets as they won't work – if using dried, it must be the soft, spongy sheets)**
- **Salt**
- **Paprika**

### BUNS/EXTRAS
- **4 vegan brioche buns spread with vegan butter**
- **1 tbsp vegan mayonnaise per bun (optional)**

## INSTRUCTIONS

### FILLING
1. If using a shop-bought vegan roast and/or shop-bought stuffing then cook them according to the instructions on the packet and serve hot.
2. If using the turkey roast from our recipe guide and our stuffing then preheat the oven to 180°C/350°F/Gas Mark 4. Place them on a baking tray with a light drizzle of oil and heat for 10 minutes or until warmed through.

### APPLE SAUCE
1. Place all the ingredients into a medium-sized saucepan on a low heat and cover with a lid.
2. Cook for around 15 minutes, stirring occasionally, until the apples break down into a purée. If the apple won't break down then pop the mixture into the food processor or blender until you reach your desired consistency. Set aside until needed.

### VEGAN CRACKLING
1. Add around 1cm of rapeseed oil to a deep frying pan or medium-sized saucepan and heat on medium-high until the oil is hot but not boiling.
2. Break the bean curd skin/yuba into palm-sized pieces and drop into the oil. They should crisp up immediately and only need a few seconds on each side.
3. Remove from the pan using a metal slotted spoon, then place on some kitchen roll and sprinkle with a tiny amount of salt and paprika. Set aside until needed.

### BUNS/EXTRAS/ASSEMBLY
1. Evenly distribute the no turkey roast slices, the stuffing, apple sauce, vegan crackling and optional vegan mayonnaise into the buttered brioche buns and serve.

# BUBBLE & SQUEAK CAKES WITH VEGAN FRIED EGGS

Prep time: **25 minutes** | Cook time: **20 minutes** | Serves: **4**

The vegan fried eggs are an added bonus as these Bubble & Squeak Cakes are delicious on their own. An easy and tasty way to use up those festive leftovers.

## INGREDIENTS

### VEGAN FRIED EGGS
### YOLKS

- 200g butternut squash, carrots or pumpkin, peeled and sliced or cut into 2cm cubes
- 1 tbsp olive oil plus extra for frying
- 2 tbsp nutritional yeast
- 2 tbsp cornflour
- 1 tbsp unsweetened plant milk
- ½ tsp black salt (Kala Namak)
- ⅛ tsp salt
- ⅛ tsp turmeric

### WHITES

- 140ml unsweetened plant milk
- 90g rice flour
- ¼-½ tsp salt
- 1 tbsp water
- 1 tbsp olive oil

### PATTIES

- 100g vegan lardons (optional)
- 1 tbsp vegan butter
- 1 white onion, finely diced
- 225g shredded savoy cabbage
- 2 cloves garlic, finely chopped
- 400g mashed potato (or about 500g raw potatoes, boiled and mashed), chilled
- 50-100g vegan cheddar-style cheese, grated (optional)
- 2 tbsp chickpea flour mixed with 2 tbsp warm water
- 1 tbsp plain flour

## INSTRUCTIONS

### VEGAN FRIED EGGS
### YOLKS

1. Boil or steam the butternut squash, carrots or pumpkin until soft. Thoroughly drain any excess water.

2. Place the steamed vegetables and the other yolk ingredients into a high-speed blender and blend until very smooth. The consistency needs to be thick and gloopy. Set aside until needed.

### WHITES

1. Using a medium-sized bowl, whisk all the ingredients together until very smooth. Set aside until needed.

### PATTIES

1. Heat a little oil in a large non-stick frying pan on a medium heat and fry the vegan lardons according to the instructions on the packet. Remove from the pan and set aside.

2. Add a tablespoon of vegan butter to the pan then add the onions and heat for 5 minutes. Add the cabbage and fry for another 5 minutes or until just wilted.

3. Stir through the garlic and heat for another 2 minutes. Remove from the heat and leave to cool slightly.

4. Using a large bowl, add the cooked vegan lardons, cooked onion, garlic and cabbage, chilled mashed potato, vegan cheese, chickpea flour mix, plain flour, wholegrain mustard, black pepper and salt. Stir all the ingredients together and then form into evenly shaped patties.

## INGREDIENTS CONT.

- **1 tbsp wholegrain mustard**
- **¼ tsp black pepper**
- **1 tsp salt**
- **Handful of fresh parsley, chopped**
- **Squeeze of lemon juice, to serve**

## INSTRUCTIONS CONT.

5. Add a little extra oil to the pan then fry the patties on a medium heat until golden, turning once.

### VEGAN FRIED EGGS (FRYING)

1. While the patties are cooking, fry the 'eggs'.

2. Using a large non-stick frying pan (with a lid), heat a little oil on medium then add 2 tablespoons of the egg white mixture. Fry for around 30 seconds.

3. Place 1 level tablespoon of the yolk mixture neatly into the centre of the white. Place the lid on and then cook for 2-3 minutes but don't flip. Remove with a spatula and cook the rest of the eggs using the same method (you might need to add a little more oil to the pan).

4. After you've mastered the technique, you can try cooking multiple eggs at the same time.

5. Serve on top of the patties.

### SERVING SUGGESTIONS
A squeeze of lemon juice, avocado salad, chutney, fresh parsley, grilled tomatoes, steamed cabbage, steamed kale

# DESSERTS

# EASY BISCOFF NO-BAKE CHEESECAKE

Prep time: **20 minutes** | Chill time: **overnight** | Serves: **10**

You won't believe how easy this cheesecake is to make and yet so divine. Golden Lotus biscuits with a fluffy, creamy centre topped with a Biscoff drizzle… well, we don't need to say anything else…

## INGREDIENTS

### BASE
- 400g Lotus Biscoff biscuits
- 150g vegan butter

### FILLING
- 200g vegan double/whippable cream
- 450g vegan plain cream cheese
- 250g Lotus Biscoff spread
- 100g icing sugar, sieved
- 3 tbsp (heaped) tbsp odourless/culinary coconut oil, melted (buy online, in health food shops and Ocado. You can use regular coconut oil but we recommend buying odourless to avoid the coconutty flavour)
- 1 tsp vanilla extract or paste
- ½ tsp salt

### TOPPING
- 150g Lotus Biscoff spread
- 50g Lotus Biscoff biscuits

### SERVING SUGGESTIONS

Dusting of icing sugar, edible flowers, freeze-dried raspberries, fresh berries, fresh mint, vegan crème fraîche, vegan honeycomb, vegan ice cream, vegan squirty cream, vegan white chocolate shavings

## INSTRUCTIONS

### BASE
1. Line a spring-form cake tin (approx. 20cm diameter and 7cm deep) with greaseproof paper.
2. Blend the Lotus Biscoff biscuits until fine or wrap in a clean tea towel and bash with a rolling pin until smooth.
3. Gently melt the vegan butter in a small saucepan on a low heat until fully dissolved. Combine thoroughly with the blended biscuits in a large mixing bowl.
4. Transfer the mixture into the lined cake tin and evenly distribute along the bottom and up the sides, packing firmly with the back of a spoon or with your hands. Place in the fridge for a minimum of 30 minutes.

### FILLING
1. Whip the vegan double cream until stiff peaks form and then place in the fridge.
2. Using a food processor or high-speed blender, thoroughly blend the vegan plain cream cheese, Lotus Biscoff spread, icing sugar, melted coconut oil, vanilla extract and salt until smooth.
3. Gently stir through the whipped vegan double cream until combined (don't overstir).
4. Pour the filling onto the base and then refrigerate overnight.

### TOPPING/ASSEMBLY
1. Once the cheesecake has chilled, place the Lotus Biscoff spread into a small saucepan and very gently heat on low until melted. If the spread gets too thick, add a couple of tablespoons of odourless coconut oil. Leave to cool then evenly pour over the top of the cheesecake.
2. Crush the Lotus Biscoff biscuits and sprinkle over the top of the cake as you like.
3. Serve immediately or return to the fridge.

# BEST EVER TIRAMISU

Prep time: **20 minutes** | Chill time: **2 hours** | Serves: **8**

Espresso soaked ladyfingers, sweet and fluffy vegan Amaretto cream with a light dusting of cocoa – mmm.

## INGREDIENTS

### SPONGE/LADYFINGERS
If you don't want to make your own, it's also possible to use 400g (approx.) Lotus Biscoff biscuits, vegan shortbread or baked French toast biscuits

### WET INGREDIENTS
- 200ml unsweetened soya or almond milk
- 75ml neutral oil (eg rapeseed)
- 2 tsp vanilla extract or paste
- 2 tsp cider vinegar

### DRY INGREDIENTS
- 200g self-raising flour
- 140g golden caster sugar
- 1 tsp baking powder
- ½ tsp salt

### ESPRESSO SYRUP
- 300ml strong coffee (6 tsp instant coffee in 300ml boiling water. Use decaffeinated if preferred)
- 1 tbsp vegan Amaretto, coffee liqueur, rum or brandy (add 2 more tablespoons if you'd prefer it extra boozy. If you'd prefer to go alcohol-free then leave out this ingredient)
- 2 tbsp caster sugar

## INSTRUCTIONS

### SPONGE/LADYFINGERS
1. Preheat the oven to 180°C/350°F/Gas Mark 4.
2. Line a 20-25cm x 30-35cm (approx.) deep baking tin.

### WET INGREDIENTS
1. In a large jug, stir together all the wet ingredients and then leave for a few minutes.

### DRY INGREDIENTS
1. In a large mixing bowl, thoroughly combine all the dry ingredients.
2. Pour the wet ingredients into the dry ingredients and stir until combined (but don't overstir).
3. Evenly distribute the cake mixture into the baking tin and place in the oven for 25 minutes.
4. Remove from the oven and leave to cool.
5. Cut the sponge into 16 even slices. Turn the slices on their side in the tin and place the tin back in the oven for 10 minutes (this is to help dry out the ladyfingers so they absorb more liquid).
6. Remove from the oven and leave to cool fully.

### ESPRESSO SYRUP
1. Using a medium-sized jug, combine all ingredients while the coffee is boiling hot then leave to cool completely.

### CREAM LAYER
1. Using an electric hand whisk or stand mixer, whisk the vegan cream until stiff peaks form.
2. In a large mixing bowl and using an electric hand whisk or balloon whisk, thoroughly combine the vegan cream cheese, icing sugar, vanilla extract, alcohol and melted coconut oil. Gently fold through the whipped vegan double cream (don't overstir).
3. Place in the fridge until needed.

## INGREDIENTS CONTS.

### CREAM LAYER
- 315ml vegan double/whippable cream
- 500g vegan cream cheese
- 190g icing sugar, sieved
- 1¼ tsp vanilla extract or paste
- 2½ tsp vegan Amaretto, coffee liqueur, rum or brandy (optional)
- 2½ tbsp odourless/culinary coconut oil, melted (optional but recommended – use this if you'd like the cream to be a bit firmer. You can use regular coconut oil but we recommend using odourless to avoid the coconutty flavour)

### TOPPING
- 2 tbsp cocoa powder or raw cacao powder
- 50g dark vegan chocolate, shaved (optional – we like 70% cocoa solids)

## INSTRUCTIONS CONTS.

### TOPPING/ASSEMBLY
1. Line a 20cm x 20cm ceramic or glass dish with greaseproof paper.
2. Dunk 8 of the ladyfingers into the espresso mixture and place in the dish in a single layer.
3. Take half the cream and spread evenly, covering the ladyfingers.
4. Take another 8 ladyfingers, thoroughly dunk them in the espresso syrup and place them over the cream, evenly spaced and in a single layer.
5. Spread the remaining half of the cream over the ladyfingers.
6. Place in the fridge and chill for a minimum of 2 hours.
7. Remove from the fridge and dust with cocoa or raw cacao powder through a sieve, then finish off with chocolate shavings.

BEST EVER
TIRAMISU

FLUFFY CHOCOLATE
MOUSSE CAKE

# FLUFFY CHOCOLATE MOUSSE CAKE

Prep time: **20 minutes** | Cook time: **25 minutes** | Chill time: **overnight** | Serves: **8**

A decadent yet light and fluffy dessert that beautifully complements a Christmas dinner. Simple to make and is sure to wow your guests – win, win!

## INGREDIENTS

### CAKE
### WET INGREDIENTS
- 130ml unsweetened soya or almond milk
- 1 tsp cider vinegar
- 40ml neutral oil (eg rapeseed)
- 1 tsp vanilla extract
- 1 tbsp golden syrup

### DRY INGREDIENTS
- 100g self-raising flour
- 35g cocoa powder
- 75g golden caster sugar
- ¾ tsp baking powder
- ¼ tsp salt

### CHOCOLATE MOUSSE
- 170g vegan dark chocolate chips or dark chocolate, broken into small pieces
- 120ml unsweetened plant milk
- 1½ tbsp odourless/ culinary coconut oil
- 235ml vegan double/whippable cream
- 3½ tbsp caster sugar
- ¼ tsp salt
- 1 tsp vanilla extract
- 1 tbsp vegan Amaretto or brandy (optional)

## INSTRUCTIONS

### CAKE
1. Preheat the oven to 180°C/350°F/Gas Mark 4.
2. Grease and line a 20cm springform cake tin with greaseproof paper.

### WET INGREDIENTS
1. In a large jug, thoroughly whisk all the wet ingredients together and set aside for 10 minutes.

### DRY INGREDIENTS
1. In a large mixing bowl, stir all the dry ingredients together.
2. Pour the wet ingredients into the bowl of dry ingredients and stir until combined (but don't overstir).
3. Pour the mixture into the cake tin. Tap the tin on the side of the work surface before placing into the oven for 20-25 minutes or until a knife comes out clean. Leave to cool completely.
4. Remove the cake from the tin, peel off the greaseproof paper then return the cake to the tin and set aside.

### CHOCOLATE MOUSSE
1. Using a microwavable bowl, add the chocolate, plant milk and coconut oil and heat in 30 second bursts. Whisk between bursts until thoroughly melted and smooth. Cool for 15 minutes (you can combine on the stovetop if preferred).
2. Thoroughly whisk the vegan cream, sugar and salt using an electric hand whisk or stand mixer until stiff peaks form.
3. Stir the vanilla extract and Amaretto or brandy (if using) into the cooled chocolate mixture then gently fold the cooled chocolate mixture into the cream until thoroughly combined and uniform in colour.
4. Pour the chocolate mousse mix into the cake tin over the cake layer and tap the tin on the work surface before placing in the fridge to set overnight.

## INGREDIENTS CONT.

### CHOCOLATE GANACHE

- 100g vegan dark chocolate chips or dark chocolate, broken into small pieces
- 100ml unsweetened plant milk

## INSTRUCTIONS CONT.

### CHOCOLATE GANACHE

1. Using a microwavable bowl, put the chocolate and plant milk in the microwave and heat in 30 second bursts. Whisk in between each burst until melted and smooth.

2. Give it a final stir then pour over the top of the cake, place in the fridge and set for an hour before serving.

**TIP**
—
If you'd prefer a more rustic-looking tart then sprinkle flaked almonds over the filling before cooking and leave off the icing.

# CLASSIC BAKEWELL TART

Prep time: **10 minutes**  |  Cook time: **45 minutes**  |  Serves: **8**

Well, who doesn't love a classic Bakewell tart – and the iconic icing of course?! It's much easier to make than it looks and we challenge you not to devour this in one sitting!

## INGREDIENTS

### PASTRY
You can also use vegan ready-to-use shortcrust pastry
- 200g plain flour
- 50g ground almonds
- 40g icing sugar
- ¼ tsp salt
- 150g vegan butter, chilled (use a vegan butter block)
- 1 tbsp ice water or vodka (vodka recommended for a flakier, more tender pastry)

### FILLING
- 250g good quality raspberry or cherry jam
- 150g ground almonds
- 3 tbsp cornflour
- 4 tbsp plain flour
- 1 tsp baking powder
- 115g caster sugar
- 85g vegan butter
- 200ml unsweetened plant milk
- 1 tsp vanilla extract
- 2 tsp almond extract
- ½ tsp salt

### DECORATION/ASSEMBLY
- 300g icing sugar, sieved
- 3 tbsp cold water
- ½ tsp almond extract
- 50g vegan dark or milk chocolate

## INSTRUCTIONS

### PASTRY
1. Grease a 25cm (approx.) loose-bottomed flan dish and set aside.
2. Using a large mixing bowl, combine all the ingredients together by hand, until the mixture forms a soft, smooth dough. Alternatively, use a food processor.
3. Form the pastry into a ball then evenly spread it onto the bottom of the greased flan dish and up the sides, ensuring there are no gaps. Prick the pastry all over with a fork, then place in the freezer for 20 minutes.
4. Preheat the oven to 180°C/350°F/Gas Mark 4.
5. Bake the tart case for 15 minutes or until just golden. Set aside to cool.

### FILLING
1. Take the cooled pastry case and evenly cover with the jam.
2. Place all the remaining filling ingredients (apart from the jam) into a food processor and blend until smooth. Pour the filling over the jam, ensuring it's evenly distributed.
3. Bake for 30 minutes or until golden and a knife comes out clean (apart from the jam!). Check after 20 minutes of baking and if it's browning too quickly, cover with foil. Remove from the oven and leave to cool completely before icing.

### DECORATION/ASSEMBLY
1. Using a large mixing bowl, add the icing sugar then stir in the almond extract and about 3 tablespoons of cold water to make a smooth, fairly thick icing. You might need a little more water but only add a tablespoon at a time.
2. Melt the chocolate using a double boiler/bain-marie and leave to cool before adding it to a piping bag without a nozzle. Set aside.
3. Evenly pour the icing over the cooled cake to the edges, without leaving any gaps.
4. Snip the very end off the piping bag and pipe parallel lines of chocolate over the white icing, then drag a cocktail stick through the lines (at a 90 degree angle to the lines) to create a feathered effect.
5. Leave to set and then serve.

# A LITTLE BIT
# EXTRA

# CHRISTMAS CAKE POPS

Prep time: **20 minutes** | Cook time: **25 minutes** | Chill time: **60 minutes**
Makes: **30 cake pops**

This recipe was inspired by fellow-foodie Rebecca Page, Charity Admin Manager and winner of Viva!'s very own staff Bake Off competition. The cake pops also make a great gift!

## INGREDIENTS

### SPONGE
### WET INGREDIENTS
- 200ml unsweetened soya or almond milk
- 75ml neutral oil (eg rapeseed)
- 2 tsp vanilla extract
- 2 tsp cider vinegar

### DRY INGREDIENTS
- 200g self-raising flour
- 140g golden caster sugar
- 1 tsp baking powder
- ¼ tsp salt

### ICING
- 40g vegan butter
- 40g vegan plain cream cheese
- 200g icing sugar, sieved
- ½ tsp vanilla extract

### CHOCOLATE COATING/ DECORATION
You will need 30 cake pop sticks – buy online
- 400g vegan chocolate of your choice (do half white, half dark if preferred)
- Vegan white fondant icing (you can leave out the white icing if preferred)
- Vegan green fondant icing
- Vegan red fondant icing
- Icing sugar (for dusting)

## INSTRUCTIONS

### SPONGE
1. Preheat the oven to 180°C/350°F/Gas Mark 4.
2. Grease and line 1 round cake tin (approx. 20cm diameter).
3. In a large jug, stir together all the wet ingredients and then leave for a few minutes.
4. In a large mixing bowl, thoroughly combine all of the dry ingredients.
5. Pour the wet ingredients into the bowl of dry ingredients and stir until combined (but don't overstir).
6. Pour the cake mixture into the tin.
7. Place the tin in the oven for 20-25 minutes or until lightly golden and a knife/skewer comes out clean. Leave to cool completely.

### ICING
1. Mix all the ingredients together until smooth.
2. Break up the cooled sponge and crumble it into the icing. Combine until you have a smooth dough.
3. Form into 20g-23g balls and then place them on a lined tray in the freezer for 30 minutes minimum.

### CHOCOLATE COATING/DECORATION
1. Melt the chocolate in 10 second bursts in the microwave or by using a double boiler/bain-marie on the stove. Leave to cool slightly.
2. Take a cake pop stick and dip the very end into the melted chocolate then push the stick into the chilled cake ball (not all the way through). Repeat this process until all the cake balls are on sticks.
3. Dip each cake pop into the melted chocolate, allowing it to drip off a little.
4. Place the pops in an upturned colander, mug, florist's foam or lollipop holder stand and then place in the fridge for 30 minutes.
5. Roll out the green and white fondant icing to around 2mm thick and use tiny Christmas pudding cutters (buy online) to create the white icing and green leaves. Use the red fondant icing to roll tiny red berries. Dust with icing sugar.

# TRADITIONAL MINCE PIES

**Prep time: 20 minutes** | **Cook time: 25 minutes** | **Makes: 16-20 pies**

Several Viva! staff members said these were the nicest mince pies they'd ever eaten. With a melt-in-your-mouth pastry and boozy, fruity centre, we have to agree!

## INGREDIENTS

### FILLING

Or use around 400g (approx.) ready-to-use vegan mincemeat

(Make the filling 1-3 days in advance)

- **1 large apple (ideally sour), peeled, cored and finely diced**
- **Juice and zest of 1 orange**
- **100g dried cranberries or sour cherries**
- **100g raisins, sultanas or currants**
- **70g candied orange peel or candied mixed peel**
- **40g flaked almonds (optional)**
- **100g light brown sugar (eg light muscovado)**
- **100g dark brown sugar (eg dark muscovado)**
- **2 tsp ground cinnamon**
- **1½ tsp ground ginger**
- **1 tsp ground nutmeg**
- **⅛ tsp allspice**
- **¾ tsp ground cloves**
- **¼ tsp ground cardamom (optional)**
- **¼ tsp salt**
- **100g vegan butter**
- **100ml vegan brandy, whisky, port or Amaretto**
- **1 tsp vanilla extract**

## INSTRUCTIONS

### FILLING

1. Using a large mixing bowl, thoroughly combine the apple, orange juice and zest, cranberries, raisins, candied peel, flaked almonds, sugar, cinnamon, ginger, nutmeg, allspice, cloves, cardamom and salt. Set aside for an hour.
2. After an hour, take a large saucepan and add the vegan butter and mincemeat filling. On a low-medium heat, simmer for around 30 minutes or until most of the liquid has evaporated and the apple is soft. Leave to cool for 20 minutes.
3. Stir through the brandy (or other liqueur) and vanilla extract, thoroughly combine then transfer to a sealed container and refrigerate until ready to use.

### PASTRY

1. Using a large mixing bowl, combine the flour and salt then add the vegetable fat/shortening and vegan butter and rub together until the mixture looks like breadcrumbs.
2. Add the sugar, plant milk and vodka and knead in the bowl until a smooth dough forms. Cover and leave to rest for 15 minutes.

## INGREDIENTS CONT.

### PASTRY

Or use a vegan ready-to-roll shortcrust pastry block

- 550g plain flour, plus extra for dusting
- ½ tsp salt
- 130g vegan white vegetable fat/shortening/baking fat, cubed
- 130g vegan butter block, cubed
- 4 tbsp caster sugar
- 2 tbsp plant milk
- 2 tbsp ice cold water or chilled vodka (we recommend using vodka for a light, flakey pastry)
- 2 tbsp unsweetened plant milk mixed with 1 tbsp syrup (eg maple or agave) for brushing

## INSTRUCTIONS CONT.

### ASSEMBLY

1. Preheat the oven to 180°C/350°F/Gas Mark 4.
2. Roll the pastry out on a floured surface to the thickness of a pound coin (3mm). You can use mini foil cases or cupcake tins. When using mini foil tins we use a 9cm diameter pastry cutter for the outer pastry layer and an 8cm diameter cutter for the lid.
3. Line the foil cases or tins with the pastry circles (you'll need to use a palette knife or sharp knife to remove the pastry from the floured surface as it's very delicate).
4. Spoon 1 tablespoon of mincemeat into each pastry base. Re-roll the pastry trimmings and cut out the lids then place over the top. Seal the pastry base with the lid using a fork around the edge. You can also add a small Christmas shape (eg star) with the excess pastry, using an additional cutter (optional).
5. Brush the pies with the soya milk/syrup mix then bake for 25 minutes or until lightly golden. Leave to cool for 10 minutes before carefully removing from the tins and transferring to a wire rack. Dust with icing sugar. Store in an airtight container for up to 3 days.

**Note:** the mince pies will be slightly crumbly until completely cooled.

### SERVING SUGGESTIONS
Fresh berries, vegan brandy butter, vegan cream, vegan crème fraîche, vegan custard, vegan ice cream

# SHARING
# DISHES

# PROSECCO FONDUE

Prep time: **10 minutes**  |  Cook time: **30 minutes**  |  Serves: **4-6**

Go Swiss this Christmas and get together with friends and family for this exquisite sharing dish – ideal for festive occasions.

## INGREDIENTS

- 350g potatoes, peeled and roughly chopped
- 125g unsalted cashews
- 1 onion, finely diced
- 3 cloves garlic, finely chopped
- 6 tbsp nutritional yeast
- 2 tsp Dijon mustard or white miso paste
- 1½ tsp salt
- ¼ tsp black pepper
- ½ tsp ground or fresh nutmeg, grated
- 1 tsp lemon juice
- 2 tbsp tapioca flour/ starch (buy in health food shops, online and in global supermarkets)
- ½ tbsp syrup (eg maple or agave)
- 250ml vegan prosecco or vegan dry white wine
- 1½ tbsp kirsch or cognac (optional)
- 150g strong vegan cheese, grated (optional)

## INSTRUCTIONS

1. In a large saucepan of boiling water, add the potatoes and cashews. Bring to the boil then simmer for 15 minutes. Drain and set aside.

2. While the potatoes and cashews are simmering, fry the onion in a little oil until golden.

3. Add the garlic and fry for a further 2 minutes.

4. Using a high-speed blender (with the largest blender jug), add the cooked potatoes, cashews, onion and garlic, along with all of the other ingredients (apart from the vegan cheese). Blend until smooth.

5. Using a large saucepan, pour in the mixture from the blender and add the vegan cheese. Bring to the boil then simmer for around 5 minutes or until the sauce thickens.

6. Either transfer the fondue to a fondue pot or serve straight from the pan.

### SERVING SUGGESTIONS
Avocado, boiled or roast potatoes, breadsticks, broccoli, cauliflower, cherry tomatoes, crusty bread pieces, gherkins, grapes, green apple pieces, mushrooms, pasta (cooked), smoked tofu cubes, tortilla chips, vegan mock meats (cooked)

# HOW TO CREATE A SPECTACULAR VEGAN CHEESEBOARD

Prep time: **15 minutes**

There are so many fabulous vegan cheeses out there now including supermarket favourites and artisan delights. There's no reason to go without your favourite blue or 'cheddar' this Christmas so get creative and have lots of fun along the way!

**STAGE ONE:** choose your favourite wooden board to showcase your 'cheese'. Adding a few small bowls or dishes can help create interest and variety. You can arrange these now, to be filled later. For an extra touch of colour and texture, we like to use dried decorative orange slices.

**STAGE TWO:** select your favourite vegan cheeses, unwrap them and spread them out around the board. Partially or fully slicing some of them adds appeal. For firmer 'cheeses' like 'cheddar', you can cut them into cubes for easy snacking.

**STAGE FOUR:** fill the gaps with fresh herbs eg rosemary sprigs. We also like to use little bunches of red currants to add some festive cheer.

**STAGE THREE:** now you can start adding your extras – it's nice to group them together for colour and pop. Select from: vibrant raspberries, blueberries, strawberries, blackberries, red grapes, oranges or satsuma segments, apple slices, dried apricots, dates, fresh figs, pomegranate, physalis, sharon fruit, olives, cherry tomatoes, cucumber, baby peppers, vegan ham, vegan chorizo, nuts, vegan caramelised nuts, a selection of crackers, pickles and chutney, gherkins or cornichons, pickled onions, pickled walnuts, kimchi, sauerkraut, maple syrup and vegan dips. At this stage, you can place some of your chosen extras in the little dishes.

**STAGE FIVE**: enjoy the sheer delight and amazement of friends and family as they tuck into your beautiful creation!

# DRINKS

# LUXURY HOT CHOCOLATE

Prep time: **5 minutes** | Cook time: **10 minutes** | Serves: **2**

Thick, velvety, chocolatey, creamy decadence in a mug – you'll be transported to the cosy cafés of Italy in one divine gulp.

## INGREDIENTS

- 170ml unsweetened plant milk
- 60ml vegan double/ whippable cream (you don't need to whip it)
- 1 tbsp high-quality cocoa powder or raw cacao powder
- 60g vegan dark chocolate (we like 70% cocoa solids but use vegan milk chocolate for kids or if you prefer a sweeter/more subtle flavour), cut into small pieces
- 2 tbsp sugar
- ⅛ tsp salt
- 2 tsp vanilla extract (you can use orange extract or mint extract as an alternative)
- 1 tbsp cornflour mixed with 60ml unsweetened plant milk
- Pinch of cinnamon
- 2 tbsp vegan Irish cream liqueur, rum, brandy, whisky or coffee liqueur (optional)

**Optional toppings:** cocoa powder, vegan mini marshmallows, vegan squirty cream

## INSTRUCTIONS

1. Using a medium-sized saucepan, heat the milk and cream on a low-medium heat for a few minutes or until warmed through.

2. Stir through the cocoa powder and whisk continuously for a minute.

3. Add the chocolate, sugar, salt and vanilla extract and bring to the boil.

4. Stir through the cornflour mix, cinnamon and alcohol. Whisk really thoroughly then immediately turn off the heat and serve.

# VEGAN IRISH CREAM LIQUEUR

Prep time: **5 minutes** | Makes: **1 litre (approx.)**

This is a delectable dairy-free homemade version of the very popular creamy alcoholic drink – we challenge you to tell the difference...

## INGREDIENTS

- 250ml Irish whiskey
- 250ml vegan double/ whippable cream (you don't need to whip it)
- 130ml unsweetened plant milk
- 370g vegan condensed milk
- 1 tbsp instant coffee mixed with 1 tbsp boiling water, left to cool
- 2 tsp vanilla extract
- 2 tbsp vegan chocolate syrup or 2 tsp cocoa powder (optional)

## INSTRUCTIONS

1. Place all the ingredients into a high-speed blender and blend until smooth.
2. Transfer to airtight sterilised storage jars or bottles and refrigerate immediately.

**TIP**

After refrigerating your Vegan Irish Cream Liqueur, it might thicken up a little bit. If this happens, just pop it back in the blender and whizz it up again.

We wish you
a very vegan
Christmas
x